SCOTTI:
UNITED
MUSEU:

Uniform
of the
Scottish
Infantry

1740 to 1900

W. A. THORBURN

Keeper Scottish United Services Museum

HMSO/EDINBURGH

ISBN 0 11 490403 0

Introduction

Although distinctive and often picturesque clothing is usually associated with soldiers it is only in comparatively modern times that uniforms have been designed, and developed in accordance with purely military fashions, and up to the end of the 18th century armies were dressed in regularised versions of civilian dress.

In earlier times, uniform as it is now understood, did not exist, and a soldier was recognisable only because he wore armour, or carried weapons, friend being distinguished from foe by the use of coloured sashes or other superficial means. Certain royal bodyguards, or groups of mercenaries who operated as disciplined bodies, tended to dress in a uniform manner, but it was not until the end of the 17th century that the national armies of Europe began to appear in clothing of a uniform colour and design, by which they could be identified, either as the army of a particular nation, or one of its sub-divisions.

The first rules for such clothing appeared in Britain about 1678, and in 1689 the British red coat had acquired the characteristics it was to have, with some modifications, well into the 18th century. In 1727 efforts were made to ensure that regiments conformed to a universal style, and that each displayed the correct facing colour or lace pattern, as the visible identity of individual units was now as important as that of the army as a whole. Although tartan is often thought to be a feature of the dress of all Scottish regiments, this was a purely Highland distinction, until the 1880s, and during most of their long existence the Lowland Scottish regiments wore exactly the same pattern of uniform as the rest of the British Army. When discussing the costume history of these, the oldest Scottish infantry formations, the development of British Army dress in general is involved. The earliest uniform coats were loose fitting, worn with broad brimmed hats, the sides of which were turned up or "cocked", developing in course of time into the formalised tricorn. About 1705 long gaiters were worn to protect breeches and stockings, and the change from matchlock to flintlock muskets, caused bandoliers with charges of loose powder to be replaced by cartridge boxes worn on shoulder belts. For nearly 150 years the flintlock musket, and its associated equipment carrying bayonet and ammunition box, was standard throughout the armies of the world.

In the 18th century the Scottish infantry regiments fought in red coats, tricorns or mitre-shaped grenadier caps, like the rest of the army, but in 1739 an important event occurred which began a unique military uniform tradition. In 1725 six Independent Companies of soldiers were raised for police duty in the Highlands of Scotland, and when they were formed into a regiment in 1739, numbered 43rd in the British Line Infantry, they were uniformed in red coats, but in conjunction with the native garb of combined kilt and plaid, called a belted plaid. This regiment, later re-numbered 42nd, was the Royal Highland Regiment or Black Watch, whose modification of the Highland dress to combine with British Army uniform, was the basis for the attire of all subsequent regiments raised in the Highlands of Scotland. The tartan worn by this famous regiment was classified as "Universal" or "Government" tartan, and as such was to become official for all Highland units. Over twenty regular, and twenty-six fencible regiments were raised in the Northern areas of Scotland between 1739 and 1800, but of these only a very small proportion continued to modern times. Of the regiments which did remain only one, the 79th, did not have either Black Watch tartan, or Black Watch with extra lines superimposed, and when in 1881, the Lowland regiments adopted a version of Highland dress, it was the Black Watch tartan which was used, although individual regimental patterns were later authorised. During the American Revolution, and on service in tropical countries, the regulation uniforms of basic European designs were radically altered to suit local conditions, but up to the French Revolution the civilian influences of the 18th century dominated the thoughts of army tailors, and a poor man could be dressed in the current style, if not the quality, of a gentleman by joining the army. However, by the end of the century purely military fashions began to circulate throughout Europe, and the national characteristics of friend and foe alike were freely copied and exchanged. By the end of the Napoleonic Wars, items of dress, and indeed whole uniforms, had begun to establish the martial trends which were to develop with increasing complexity for the next hundred years, and which, with the inevitable variations brought about by the passage of time, were to survive into the 20th century as an easily recognised aspect of national costume. In 1800 the very military shako with its eye-shade, or peak, and metal badge replaced the long familiar cocked hat, and in 1808 the last connection with the previous century disappeared when, to the delight of all, the practice of wearing the hair in a greased queue was ended. Long-tailed coats gave way to closer

fitting short jackets, and trousers replaced breeches and gaiters, causing the soldier to assume a national, and regimental character of his own, less dominated by civilian fashion and more by experience of war, and by imitation of the troops of other lands.

By 1809 six of the existing Highland regiments did not wear Highland dress, but were attired in ordinary infantry uniform, and those who continued to use the national dress, did so in a form which had changed with the times. The full belted plaid gave way in 1810 for all purposes, to the Feileadh Beag, or little kilt, and the bonnet was now decorated with so many feathers that they were the most obvious feature.

Previously Highland Corps had worn a modified shortened form of the long red coat, but now they were able to wear virtually the same uniform as other regiments, except for the kilt, and feathered head-dress.

The most flamboyant period in the history of uniform was between 1816 and the Crimean War, and in the years following the defeat of Napoleon military elegance was at its height. Few British uniforms were ever designed without obvious foreign influence, and the regulations of 1816 and 1822 dressed the infantry according to the spectacular standards of the French and Prussians. Lack of active service reduced the serviceability of clothing design, and the long tailed coat re-appeared in 1820; officers uniforms although more standardised by 1822, were heavily decorated with gold lace, and head-dresses became more elaborate and less practical.

Highland units fully participated in the new craze for stylish uniforms, and it is interesting to note that Highland dress worn by civilians from this period onwards has been mainly based on the dress of the Highland regiments, and not as might be expected, the other way round, and changes in civilian design usually followed those of the army.

4

After 1830 the exaggerations were not quite so marked, but three of the Highland regiments which had lost their Highland dress regained it, between 1824 and 1864. They did not wear the kilt, however, but tartan trousers or "trews". The 71st for instance had a very distinctive appearance as a Highland light infantry regiment, in diced shakos, tartan trousers, and plaids; the officers being armed with Highland broadswords and dirks.

In 1842 the army was issued with percussion muskets, but went to the Crimean War in uniforms very little changed from those of the Napoleonic Wars, in fact they had been made less suitable for war by the long period of peace, and concentration on parade ground appearances.

In 1855 radical changes took place, and as in most other armies at this time, French styles were copied. A new double-breasted tunic replaced the old coatee, worn in the form of a doublet in the Highland regiments, and the characteristic French 1842 pattern tapered shako became the standard infantry headgear.

The double-breasted tunics and doublets only lasted one year, similar single-breasted garments taking their place, in 1856. The completely French head-dress was altered in detail as those in France did so, but after 1870, a spiked helmet of German origin was adopted, the full dress tunic also becoming more Prussian in design.

In the 1870s a period of Colonial warfare began, causing experiments to be made with equipment and dress more suitable for service in hot climates. Officially red was still worn in service dress order, but as early as 1846 Indian troops had worn earth coloured clothing, and during the Kaffir, Abyssinian and Afghan Wars of 1851, 1868, and 1879, khaki or drab uniforms were worn by British regiments.

In 1881 important re-organisation took place, and regiments over the number 25 were amalgamated in pairs, forming the Lowland and Highland regiments whose titles were to continue as household names in Scotland, up to the major reductions and amalgamations announced in 1957.

As a result of the 1881 reforms the Scottish infantry consisted of 9 two-battalion regiments, and 1 of one battalion, exclusive of the Scots Guards, which had always been a separate corps as the 3rd Regiment of Foot Guards.

Three of the Lowland regiments, Royal Scots, Royal Scots Fusiliers and King's Own Scottish Borderers, were not amalgamations, but continuations of the old 1st, 21st and 25th Regiments of Foot. The fourth, the Cameronians, was a combination of the 26th Foot and the 90th Perthshire Light Infantry, unique in its new form, as Scotland's only Rifle Regiment dressed in the green uniform peculiar to this arm of the service.

All the Highland regiments were amalgamations except the Cameron Highlanders, having titles instead of the numbers of their component units. The senior of these became the 1st Battalions of the new regiments, and for some time the two battalions continued to wear the dress distinctions of the old regiments. In due course, however, one uniform was used by both, cherished features and parts of insignia being incorporated into a new regimental tradition.

Pipers have always been associated with Scottish regiments, but it is seldom realised that it was not until 1854 that they were given official sanction.

Even so, this applied only to certain Highland regiments; the 73rd, 75th, and 91st Regiments were not included, and no Lowland units were considered.

Up to this date pipers had been maintained at the expense of the Colonel, their existence was not recognised by the War Office, and no reference to their uniforms can be found in official regulations.

In 1881 each Highland regiment was allowed five pipers but as late as 1884 Lowland regiments were only permitted to have a similar five, if they were not

5

charged to public funds, and it was not until 1918 that all Scottish regiments were authorised to have one pipe-major and six pipers, any extra still to be at regimental expense.

Despite the difficulties, and outright rules to the contrary, efforts were always made to keep pipers, and in fact while the 91st and 92nd, two Highland regiments, were being forbidden to have pipers in 1852, the 25th and 26th, two Lowland units, contrived to justify theirs, although at the expense of the officers.

It has become normal for all Scottish regiments, whether Highland or Lowland, to have pipers, those of Lowland corps wearing Highland dress for a long time, and the pipes and drums of any regiment are possibly the most popular image of the Scottish soldier, although except in the case of Highlanders, the dress has

been artificially applied, and originally had nothing to do with the regimental uniform as such.

The adoption of semi-Highland dress, and pipers in full Highland dress, by Lowland regiments, has done much to create the mistaken modern impression that this is a traditional Scottish national costume, when in fact it was the distinction of regiments raised in the Highlands, or specifically classed as Highland. The military development of this dress, however, virtually created a national costume, and gave the British Army its only completely native uniform, based on the apparel of part of these islands, not on the influence of foreign fashion, or on service conditions abroad. The following illustrations of changes in uniform are all from contemporary sources in the Museum collection.

1. 26th Regiment 1742

The first reliable contemporary illustrations of British private soldiers were engravings published in 1742, this example showing the 26th Cameronians. The coat was red with yellow facings, equipment being of buff leather. A shoulder belt supported an ammunition pouch, on the front of which was a pricker and brush for cleaning the touch holes and priming pans of flintlock muskets. As bayonets were of the socket type with no grip, a short sword was also carried. Tricorn hats were standard military headgear, but grenadiers were distinguished by mitre-shaped caps.

2. Black Watch 1743

3. 25th Regiment 1773

The unusual appearance of Highland
soldiers attracted the attention of British
and foreign artists in the 18th century,
this engraving by G. Bickham being an
example. It illustrates the short Highland
jacket without lapels, with small turned up
cuffs displaying the facing, or distinctive,
colour. At this period the colour was buff,
blue not being adopted until 1758 when
the regiment became Royal Highlanders.
Bonnets were of plain blue cloth without
dicing, this later feature being a decorative
development of the functional coloured
tape used to adjust the size of the bonnet.
Weapons and equipment were British
Army issue, with the addition of broadsword, dirk, and Highland pistol. Tartan
was the military pattern, later known as
Black Watch, or 42nd tartan.

This watercolour is one of a series painted
when the 25th, King's Own Scottish
Borderers, were in Minorca between 1769
and 1775. Soldiers on foreign service
frequently adapted regulation dress to
local conditions, or had to wear modified
old clothing. In this instance the coat may
be a shortened version of an old one,
but light companies were issued with
short coats, and gaiters in 1771. The
tricorn hat was losing its original shape
at this period, this somewhat mis-shaped
version being in keeping with the soldier's
general appearance. Blankets were
carried "bandolier fashion", knapsacks
were made of goatskin, and in 1767 white
gaiters were replaced by black ones for
all occasions.

4. 25th Regiment 1773

This illustration from the Minorca series shows a private of the grenadier
company in full dress. The shoulder decorations, and fur caps which had now
replaced mitre caps, were grenadier distinctions, as were match cases on shoulder
belts although these were no longer used for igniting grenades. Belts became
much narrower in the 1760s and the strap over the right shoulder was intended
as a waist-belt, but the practice of wearing both bayonet and cartridge pouch
on crossed belts was gaining favour in all European armies.

5. Royal Scots 1792

This print by Hodges after Dayes depicts an officer wearing the final development of 18th century uniform. The old knee length coats with turnbacks had now been replaced by tailed coats cut with a curve to expose the waistcoat, and gold lace buttonholes adorned the lapels. Larger and more elaborate hats were decorated with feathers and short black gaiters replaced the long white or black type. This officer wears a gorget at his neck, which shows he is an officer on duty.

6. Black Watch 1790

This watercolour by Edward Dayes, draughtsman to the Duke of York, shows a soldier of the regiment. It appears to represent a Sergeant, broadswords having been given up by men below this rank in 1776. Black belts had previously been worn, but these were changed to white in 1789. White waistcoats were in use from 1768, and bonnets were now more firmly set-up, with red, green, white, dicing. The origin of the later feathered bonnet is evident, decoration at this time consisting of a small piece of fur, or cluster of feathers. Privates wore goatskin or leather sporrans, but sergeants and officers provided themselves with more elaborate designs. The Museum has a companion picture which depicts an officer at the same period.

7. Scots Guards 1792

In the year when this print was published, sergeants of the Foot Guards exchanged their halberds for pikes, a halberd being carried by this Sergeant of the 3rd Foot Guards. The laced button holes were placed in threes, the spacing of buttons being a means of recognising the different regiments of Foot Guards to the present day. An Order of 1790 removed lace from the brims of Guardsmen's hats, but feather plumes were authorised. Plume colours varied, but at this period Scots Guards sergeants had white. After 1796 only flank companies wore white or green plumes, the rest having white and red.

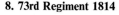

8. 73rd Regiment 1814

Although this print was published in 1814
it illustrates the radical changes begun in
1796. The waistcoat was no longer visible,
and this officer wears the typical double-
breasted jacket, which could be worn
either buttoned over, or with the lapels
showing. Hats were replaced by shakos
about 1800, this being the 1812 model.
The regiment was formed from the 2nd
Battalion Black Watch, existing as a
separate corps from 1786, and wearing
ordinary Line uniform with green
facings. In 1881 it was amalgamated with
the Black Watch, again becoming their
2nd Battalion in Highland dress.

9. Black Watch 1808

This print was published in 1808, but
shows the dress of Highland officers
throughout the Napoleonic Wars. The
jacket was virtually the same as other
infantry, worn with a wide sword belt
with regimental plate on front. Sashes
were worn over the left shoulder and
commissioned ranks now had elaborate
sporrans of a regimental pattern. The
traditional broadsword was now a
regulation model with a brass hilt, and
the bonnet, although still the same head-
dress as before, was now so heavily
decorated with black feathers that quite
a new aspect resulted. The 42nd Regiment,
or Black Watch, displayed a red hackle
plume, those of other Highland Corps
being white and red.

10. Scots Guards 1815

One of the best contemporary prints of
British infantry uniform worn during the
Waterloo campaign, from a drawing by
the French military artist Carle Vernet.
Breeches and gaiters had been replaced
by blue grey trousers, and the short,
close fitting jacket, with cross-belt equipment, was standard throughout the Army.
This illustration shows a corporal of the
grenadier company 3rd Foot Guards in
marching order, which on active service
was the same as Line regiments. Guards
still retained white breeches, cocked hats,
or grenadier caps for home cremonial,
but unlike the French Guards they did
not take full dress to the battlefield.

11. 92nd Regiment 1815

A coloured engraving from a drawing by
Finart which clearly illustrates the
Highland version of uniform as worn by
privates during the Napoleonic Wars.
Jackets and equipment were the same as
other regiments, and peaks, like those
on shakos were added to feathered
bonnets during the Peninsular War. The
belted plaid had gone, and the kilt was
now a short garment finishing at the
waist. No sporrans were worn by
Highlanders on active service, and short
grey gaiters protected the lower leg and
hose from wet and mud. The facings of
this regiment The Gordon Highlanders,
were yellow, the tartan being Black Watch
with a yellow line added.

12. Black Watch 1822

The uniforms of Highland regiments
followed the general trend towards
elaboration after Waterloo. The first
official Dress Regulations for officers
of the Army appeared in 1822, and
although these laid down precise rules
for regimental dress, they were unable to
deal fully with the increasing individuality
of Highland Corps. An attempt was made,
as in the past, to relate all such regiments
to the 42nd, causing confusion in matters
of detail. This drawing by Heath shows
that Highlanders wore the current style;
the shoulder wings, however, do not
necessarily indicate a flank company,
as all 42nd officers wore them at this
period. Sporrans and dirks were of
regimental pattern, brass hilted swords
being changed to steel in 1828.

13. 25th Regiment 1826

After the final defeat of Napoleon
uniforms became more elaborate, and
this drawing of an officer by H. Heath
demonstrates the influence of foreign
fashions. The shako, introduced in 1816,
of the type worn by the French and
Germans, and a more formalised braided
front to the coat, were notable features.
The short jackets, developed during the
years of active service, gave way again to
long-tailed coats, and epaulettes became
very large and heavy. At first collars with
V-shaped openings were retained, but a
closed Prussian type was adopted about
1820. Sleeves were very tight, but
trousers were made much wider. Regimental devices on belt and shako plates were
now given more attention than before.

Officer, B₂
25ᵗ Foot. In

14. Royal Scots 1838

In 1829 lapels on officers' coats were
abolished, only two rows of buttons
remaining. The high Prussian collar was
retained, but heavily decorated with two
loops of regimental lace. From 1830
gold lace distinguished regular units,
silver being confined to Militia. In the
same year gorgets were discontinued, and
in 1835 ball tufts replaced feather plumes
on shakos which were still what are normally called "bell-tops". This print
published in 1838 shows gilt chin-scales;
in 1839 these were replaced by leather
straps, although brass, or gilt, chains
were adopted after a short period.
Trousers were dark grey cloth with a
narrow red stripe, although white linen
was used for summer wear.

15. 75th Regiment 1835

Raised in 1787 the 75th were designated
a Highland regiment, but lost this distinction in 1809, after which they wore
ordinary infantry uniform. This print,
from a series illustrating military costume
between 1833 and 1840, depicts an officer
of the grenadier company, identified by
wings instead of epaulettes, and a bearskin cap. The cap has a gilt plate above
the peak which indicates a date no later
than 1835 when this was removed. The
sword pattern shown remained unaltered
between 1822 and 1895. In 1862 the title
"Stirlingshire" was added to the number,
and in 1881 on amalgamation with 92nd,
the 75th became 1st Gordon Highlanders.

16. 26th Regiment 1835

17. 72nd Regiment 1854

Officers had worn blue frock coats as
an undress uniform for some time, and
in 1828 an official pattern was authorised.
This was single breasted with a Prussian
collar, worn with a sash and black
sword belt. The coat is described in the
1834 regulations as having eight buttons,
Highland regiments wearing gilt crescents
on the shoulder straps with an
embroidered thistle. This coat was
abolished in 1848, but reintroduced as
a double breasted garment in 1852. The
wide topped diced forage cap with a
black leather peak was introduced in
1831, but in 1852 a smaller version
appeared with a very narrow top. Certain
regiments were allowed to wear badges
on these, but the 26th Cameronians
continued to use the number only.

One of a series of prints published in
1854 which shows the non-kilted
Highland uniform of the mid-19th
century. The regiment was created in
1778 as the 78th Highlanders, the number
being changed to 72nd in 1786. In 1809,
on the loss of Highland identity, ordinary
infantry dress was issued, but in 1823
the Highland character was restored on
the re-adoption of tartan, this time in the
form of trews of Prince Charles Edward
Stewart tartan, a similar design to Royal
Stewart. Another regiment, raised in
1793, had been named 78th Highlanders,
and in 1881 it amalgamated with the
72nd to form the Seaforth Highlanders,
the new regiment wearing the Mackenzie
kilt of the 78th.

18. 90th Light Infantry 1850

This is the light infantry plate of a series of prints after the drawings of M. A. Hayes.
Minor alterations were made to the same plate to show different regiments. This specimen
represents the 90th, the only Lowland light infantry regiment. The earliest date is 1844,
as the head-dress worn is the so-called Albert shako introduced in that year, although it
had been authorised in December 1843. The soldier in the centre is using his ramrod,
in the process of loading the percussion musket adopted in 1842. Light regiments wore
the same uniform as ordinary infantry, but were distinguished by bugle-horn badges, and
by shoulder wings like the flank companies of other regiments. White trousers were
abolished in 1846, except for hot climates abroad, blue being worn at home. In 1881
the 90th (Perthshire) Light Infantry were linked with the 26th Cameronians to form the
Scottish Rifles.

19. 79th Regiment 1837

As in other cases the heading date is, or close to, the year of publication of
the print, but the dress worn to 1855 is shown here. As the subject is a
battalion officer of the Cameron Highlanders he wears fringed epaulettes,
and the sporran in use at this period is clearly shown. Hackle plumes were
red and white before 1829, after which they were white. In 1834 the bonnet
was 13 inches tall, the plume 8 inches, although in fact much longer plumes
were normally used. In 1847 officers' bonnets were increased to 16 inches.

20. 93rd Regiment 1855

After the Crimean War the coatee was abolished to be replaced by a double-breasted tunic with long skirts. The Highland version had separate flaps, two in front and two at the back, designed to accommodate the sporran. Epaulettes were abolished, and badges of commissioned rank were worn on the collar. Shoulder belts were also discontinued in non-Highland corps, swords being transferred to waist belts with slings. The double-breasted tunic and Highland doublet were replaced by single-breasted versions in 1856.

21. 91st Regiment 1854

This regiment was raised in 1794 as
the 98th Argyllshire Highlanders, the
number changing to 91st in 1798.
Highland identity was lost in 1809, but
restored in 1864, with a partial return to
Highland dress. This pencil sketch by
D. Cunliffe is dated 1854, although the
obsolescent cross belts are still shown.
The subject is a private of the grenadier
company with shoulder wings, and white
shako pompon. Grenadier and light
companies were abolished between 1859
and 1860. The 91st and 93rd were linked
in 1881 to form the 1st and 2nd Battalions
of Argyll and Sutherland Highlanders.

22. 93rd Regiment 1852

A watercolour painted in Portsmouth in
1852 showing the uniform of the
Sutherland Highlanders just before and
during the Crimean War. In 1822 all
members of this regiment were ordered
to wear shoulder wings, a feature
normally confined to the grenadier and
light companies, the jacket illustrated
being the one approved in 1836. Collar
and cuffs displayed yellow facings;
the regimental sporran with brass rimmed
top was introduced about 1830. Feathered
bonnets were twelve inches high for
battalion companies, while those of
grenadiers were fourteen inches.
Cross-belt equipment was changed in
1852, so that bayonets were worn on a
waistbelt, and white spats, which had
originated about 1823, were now worn
by all Highlanders.

23. 72nd Regiment 1856

One of a number of photographs, taken at Queen Victoria's suggestion, of soldiers who had served in the Crimea. They wear the double-breasted doublets, withdrawn in 1856 or the following year, diamond shaped buttons being peculiar to Highland uniform. Beards were permitted in the Crimea, the only time this has been allowed except in the case of pioneers and some pipe-majors. Private Harper, on the right, wears an undress bonnet with light company bugle badge.

24. Scots Guards 1859

Private W. Reynolds, a native of Edinburgh, who won the Victoria Cross at the Battle of Alma in 1854. He wears the 1852 equipment, and the 1856 single-breasted tunic; the pouch on his shoulder belt contains percussion caps for the 1853 Enfield Rifle. A bearskin cap was worn in full dress, but a stiffened blue undress cap, with a diced band, was used for other occasions. The illustration is from an oil painting owned by the Regiment, a reproduction of which they presented to the Museum.

25. 92nd Regiment 1861

Representatives of the Depot Company including officers and NCOs, photographed at
Stirling. A boy drummer, and the bearded pioneer sergeant appear in the rear row.
At this time Highland and other British uniform had assumed the main characteristics
it was to keep until the decline of full dress, although several changes of detail occurred.
After 1866 a Snider breech-loading modification of the Enfield Rifle was issued,
and in 1875 a completely new design of equipment was introduced. From 1868 the shape
of the cuff was altered, in the case of Highlanders a gauntlet type was chosen, other
infantry having a pointed cuff, to which a trefoil was added.
The last of the three French pattern shakos was worn from 1869 which was lower than
the original model, and had brass chin chains. A spiked helmet of German origin was the
subject of experiment from 1876, a satisfactory British design being issued to the infantry
between 1878 and 1881; this innovation did not of course affect the Highland bonnet.
During this period, the old hard tartan was replaced by a much softer cloth, a change
intended to improve the comfort of the soldiers, as the soft material was less likely to
injure the knees of Highlanders, especially while marching in wet, cold weather.

26. Bandsman and Band Sergeant 1877

27. Gordon Highlanders 1885

The uniform of bandsmen is illustrated in a watercolour of the Royal Scots by R. Simkin. The dress was virtually the same as the rest of the regiment, with the addition of wings, previously the distinction of flank companies. The photograph of the Gordons shows a development of the 1875 valise equipment, diced glengarries being used in several orders of dress instead of feathered bonnets. Sergeants wore special sporrans, and were armed with sword bayonets and short rifles: drummers had regimental doublets embellished with their own lace pattern. The figure on the right had the rank of "drummer", but bugles had replaced drums for field and barrack calls.

28. Scottish Rifles 1885

The first uniform of the Cameronians
as a rifle regiment included a green
spiked helmet of the new model. Black
Watch tartan trousers were worn up to
1892 when Douglas tartan was authorised.
At the same time this regiment reverted
to the 1869 shako, a head-dress they used
as long as full dress was worn. This
NCO has rank equivalent to Company
Colour Sergeant, in the case of rifle
regiments the arm badge included crossed
swords and bugles instead of flags.
The rifle shown is a Martini-Henry,
introduced in 1871, but not on general
issue until 1874. Equipment belts were
black leather and the green doublet
had black buttons.

29. Royal Scots Fusiliers 1895

The 21st Regiment raised very strong
objections to the imposition of tartan,
and when they finally agreed they soon
added a blue line to the universal sett,
creating a tartan of their own. This
photograph is an excellent illustration
of the Highland doublet worn by Lowland
units, although the head-dress has nothing
to do with Scottish dress as such. It is
the final version of the grenadier type
cap always worn by all fusilier regiments.
This pattern was made of bear or racoon
skin and prominently displayed the
fusilier grenade, which emblem also
adorned the collar. This sergeant wears his
crimson sash, and is in guard order.

30. Highland Light Infantry 1895

The amalgamation of the 71st and 74th
in 1881, virtually continued the existence
of the 71st H.L.I. as a non-kilted Highland
regiment. This soldier wears the distinctive
regimental version of the shako, retained
instead of the helmet. In 1888, Slade
Wallace equipment superseded the 1875
type, and in 1892 Lee-Metford magazine
rifles made their appearance. These
were changed for Lee-Enfields in 1895,
external features, however, being almost
identical.
Trousers of Mackenzie tartan had been
worn by the 71st from 1834, and these
were continued after 1881; the transforma-
tion of Lowland uniform unfortunately
tended to deprive this Highland regiment
of much of its unique appearance.

31. Seaforth Highlanders 1895

The final version of Highland full
dress, which lasted until 1914. At this
period a low collar was still in general
use, a lighter closed type being the
main minor alteration after 1900. Although
all kilted regiments wore a similar
uniform, they varied very considerably
in detail, including sporran, method of
pleating the kilt, and number of "tails"
on the bonnet, in addition to tartan,
hose, facing colours and insignia. The
"fly plaid" was a relic of the more
ancient garment, but was by this time
only a decorative feature.
This sergeant wears the Mackenzie
tartan of the old 78th, and like all
Highland regiments other than the
Black Watch a white plume decorates
the bonnet.

32. Scottish Rifles 1892

This photograph shows Highland dress
as worn by pipers of Lowland regiments.
The general appearance was similar to
Highlanders, including the glengarry,
the only pipers to use feathered bonnets
at this period being those of the
Black Watch. When the Scottish Rifles
were formed in 1881 pipers wore flat
bonnets and Black Watch tartan
trousers, changed in 1887 to glengarries
and kilts. Doublets were dark green, with
black belts; plaids and kilts were of
Douglas regimental tartan, previously
worn by the unofficial pipers of the 26th
Regiment. This subject is identified as
the Pipe Major by four chevrons and a
crown on his right sleeve.

33. Highland Light Infantry 1900

During the South African War, drab, or
khaki, uniforms replaced regimental
dress in all units, but as these were still
experimental many variations occurred.
In 1899 the H.L.I. wore the tartan
trousers shown in this sketch by H. C.
Chrisey, but by 1900 these were being
replaced by khaki. Felt hats turned up
on the left were issued for a time, but
by September 1900 covered helmets
were worn by all ranks of this regiment.
Ammunition pouches became less
common, and bandoliers of numerous
designs were used instead. Kilted
regiments wore the same drab dress but
retained their kilts which were, however,
covered by khaki aprons to remove the
contrast between tartan and the rest of
the uniform.

Conclusion

As we have seen, uniform design was affected by service conditions and changes in methods of warfare, and by 1890 it became obvious that some permanent, inconspicuous campaign dress was necessary.

The first use of uniform was to distinguish bodies of troops from their opponents, and by increasingly complicated systems, to identify the units of each army. In battle it became important to present an imposing array of well-drilled men, and in peace the more colourful the clothing the more soldierly the wearer appeared to be. He was not trained to hide himself, but to ensure that the enemy was aware of his presence, and to remain conspicuously steady under fire, either in defence or attack, and the outcome of a battle could be influenced by the disciplined deportment of the troops engaged.

More efficient firarms produced the greatest change in attitude, and it became desirable to remain out of sight for as long as possible, or wear clothing which merged with the country-side.

Better methods of communication, and more scientific assessment of terrain made it less important for commanders to personally see their armies drawn up for formal battle, and a theatrical series of movements executed by well-dressed troops did little to impress an entrenched enemy armed with magazine rifles, or automatic weapons.

The lesson was driven home during the South African War at the turn of the century, and in 1902 khaki was ordered to be the universal colour for service dress to be worn for all but ceremonial occasions.

Scottish regiments still retained their distinctive appearance in kilt or trews with the new drab uniform, and on home stations the scarlet regimental uniforms reached their highest standard of smartness and quality of manufacture.

Between the beginning of the 18th century and the end of Queen Victoria's reign the Scottish regiments of the British Army gained a reputation as fighting men unsurpassed anywhere in the World, a reputation they were to enhance during the trials of the major wars which lay ahead.

Their dress has always aroused interest wherever they have served, and although other regiments have proud histories, the Scottish dress has often been the focal point of British military prowess in the eyes of allies and enemies alike.

There never has been any glamour in the business of war itself, but the uniforms of soldiers were once the most picturesque of all male fashions, and in the study of costume they cannot be ignored. A memory of their splendour is a bright dash of colour in the troubled history of the World.

Printed in Scotland for Her Majesty's Stationery Office
by Robert MacLehose & Co., Renfrew Dd 630383/2106
K80/53-2565 8/80